Tony and Tessa were in Wellington Square.
They were looking at the statue of
the Duke of Wellington.
They did not have a thing to do.

'Look at the paint,' said Tony.
'Yes, there are two tins of paint here,' said Tessa.

'We could paint,' said Tony.
'What could we paint?' said Tessa.

'We could paint this wall,' said Tony.
'We could paint a rainbow on the wall,' said Tessa.

Tessa picked up a tin.
'This is red paint,' she said.
Tony picked up a tin with yellow paint in.

They began to paint the wall.
Tessa painted with the red paint.
Tony painted with the yellow paint.

They made a rainbow on the wall.
It was red and yellow.

Tony and Tessa looked at the rainbow.
'It is a good painting,' said Tony.
'Yes, it is lovely,' said Tessa.

Mr Miller opened the door of his shop.
'Look out,' said Tony.

Mr Miller wanted to get his tins of paint.
He looked at the wall.
He looked at the red and yellow rainbow.

'My wall! My paint!' he shouted.
'Who painted my wall?'

People ran out.
They looked at the wall.
The people looked at the lovely rainbow.

Mr Miller was cross.
The people smiled.
'Did you do this?' they said.
'Did you paint this lovely rainbow?'

'Yes, I did.
I painted it.
I painted the lovely rainbow,' said Mr Miller.

Tony and Tessa were playing by the shed.
'We could get the tins of paint,' said Tony.
'We could paint the shed,' said Tessa.
They smiled, but not for long.

'No!' shouted Fred.
'You are not going to paint my shed.'
Fred ran out of his shed.
Tony and Tessa ran off!